I0116467

Lorikeet's Crown a King
Second Edition

Rainbow Lorikeets are so full of life, their fun-loving, mischievous nature is captivating.

This story, the seventh in the Lorikeet's Book Series for young readers, is based on a family of Lorikeets who believe they are different and become Royalty by being brave and standing up to Lawrence, the bossy resident Rainbow Lorikeet.

Through my words and the creative vision of Lillian Falzon, whose illustrations brought these characters to life, I hope you enjoy a peek into the adventures of this quirky, colourful family.

Winter is getting close, the days are becoming colder and the usual diet of seeds, blossom and fruit on the trees is becoming scarce.

Lawrence the Rainbow Lorikeet takes his partner, Loretta, and his grown family almost every day to the garden where he had found the trays of sunflower seeds supplied by the resident human.

It is rare for Lawrence and his family to be the only Lorikeets in the garden now that the news of the delicious sunflower seeds has spread to other Lorikeet families.

Lawrence as usual is being "Mister Bossy Boots" and won't share his tray of seeds with anyone other than Loretta, especially now with food being scarce.

On the odd occasion Lawrence allows one of his children, who are now mature Lorikeets, to join them.

The other family's chicks have grown into magnificent adult Lorikeets.

One in particular is Royce, who visits the garden frequently with his partner Rosanna and their family.

Royce and his family are patient and perch in the trees close by waiting for a vacant tray.

Royce believes his family is from a royal line of Rainbow Lorikeets.

He has a set of rules and standards for his family to follow and finds it hard to accept the bullying, unruly, selfish behaviour Lawrence displays.

Royce has seen Lawrence upset others and feels he is now mature enough to speak with Lawrence, Lorikeet to Lorikeet.

Today, Royce's eyes shine through his blue crown, he puffs out his brilliant red and gold chest and shakes his green cloak with the red and gold lining.

Royce turns to Rosanna for the nod of approval, takes a deep breath and flies to the tray where bossy Lawrence and his partner Loretta are.

Immediately Lawrence stands tall, puffs out his chest, puts his head down and lurches at Royce letting him know he is not welcome on the tray.

Royce knows what to expect and stands his ground. Royce lurches back at Lawrence screeching and hopping toward him.

It is obvious to Royce, Lawrence does not want to speak with him.

Royce cannot back down now as he feels the eyes of the other Lorikeet families in the garden watching him to see what will happen.

Royce was only going to have a chat with Lawrence but now finds himself competing for the role of "Leader of the Lorikeets".

With this in mind, Royce stretches his wings and stands tall. Again, Royce lurches at Lawrence who steps back.

Lawrence screeches, both he and Loretta fly to another tray where Lawrence bows his head, knowing he has been defeated in the eyes of his family and the other Lorikeet families in the garden.

Royce is recognised by the other Rainbow Lorikeets as the Lorikeet willing to stand up to "Bossy Lawrence".

The Lorikeet families congratulate Royce and a huge celebration is held in his honour.

The Lorikeets agree Royce should be crowned, "King of Lorikeets".

King Royce lets out a whistle.

Rosanna, the Queen of Lorikeets and the chicks:
Princess's Rita and Rose and Prince's, Rory and Ryan
join him on the tray singing, chirping and congratulating
him on his bravery against such a fierce leader.

Now that Royce has been crowned King of the Lorikeets, he promises to maintain peace and harmony in the garden with no more bullying and unruly behaviour.

Lorikeet's Crown a King

ISBN

978-1-7642196-3-1 (Paperback)

978-1-7642196-4-8 (eBook)

www.ingramcontent.com/pod-product-compliance
Lightning Source LLC
Chambersburg PA
CBHW060841270326
41933CB00002B/163